FROM THE FOUNDERS OF

Female *invest*

Your Financial *Planner*

REVIEW • PLAN • REFLECT

Contents

"The first step? Getting your finances in order. Because the minute you do that, you open up space, time, and resources to create a life aligned with your values."

— KATIE DONEGAN —
Cofounder of the Rebel Finance School

Note to the reader

This financial planner is designed for women and nonbinary people who want to achieve financial independence. However, anyone who supports the goal of closing the financial gender gap is welcome to use it.

If you've read our first two books, *Girls Just Wanna Have Funds—a Feminist Guide to Investing* and *Girls Just Wanna Have Impact Funds,* this book serves as a helpful next step toward financial freedom. If you've just come across us, welcome to our really practical guidance on taking control of your finances. We recommend you go do the exercises and tasks in the order they are presented here.

We believe everyone has the right to financial independence, and our planner is just one way in which you can achieve this goal. This planner is for you. You deserve to be part of the changes you want to see in the world.

Planning
is power

They say that "money is power," but true mastery of this power lies not just in having money but in strategic financial planning. This will act as a compass, guiding you toward financial independence.

Think of it this way: would you embark on a journey without a map? Financial planning is your map, showing you the best ways to grow your money and achieve your goals, while avoiding unexpected debt, expenses, and missed investment opportunities.

With proper financial planning, you can enjoy a worry-free life, take care of your loved ones, and pursue your passions. Remember that financial planning is not just powerful; it's empowering. It leads to financial independence and endless possibilities.

Think of this planner as your personal finance playground—a space where knowledge holds the key to empowerment, and each step takes you closer to financial freedom.

A guided journey through *financial understanding*

When starting your financial journey, you need to take focused and consistent steps and be committed to making positive changes to your money management that will help you achieve your financial goals.

We want to provide you with the knowledge and tools you need to confidently manage your money and empower you to take charge of your financial present and future.

Think of this planner as your personal finance playground—a space where knowledge holds the key to empowerment, and each step you take moves you closer to the realm of financial freedom.

Navigating life's surprises

Life has ups and downs, and financial planning helps you be prepared for unexpected events. By understanding your own finances and having a F*** You Fund, you can confidently face unexpected events without causing stress or financial strain.

Financial planning is crucial for achieving goals, but it also reduces stress, positively impacting your relationships and well-being.

Part 1

Dream it; define it: *six steps to plan for the year ahead*

The foundation of financial success involves reviewing your financial journey from the previous year and strategically planning for the year ahead. The process unfolds through six distinct steps, which we will delve in to one by one in this section.

STEP 1
Review your financial year

STEP 2
Write down your money story

STEP 3
Envision your dream life

STEP 4
Set your financial goals

STEP 5
Identify your financial habits

STEP 6
Create your budget

Step 1: *Review your financial year*

Before you start planning for the year ahead, begin by taking a bird's-eye view of your finances over the past year. This means looking at every aspect—from the money you earned to every penny spent. It will soon become clear to you how well you are handling your money.

To get an overview of your past year's finances, start by reviewing all income sources and expenditures. Consolidate your bank statements, credit card bills, and investments. Calculate your yearly earnings, then categorize your expenses, noting your essential expenditure as well as any discretionary spending. Were there any surprise costs? Did you stick to a budget?

Reflect on your financial peaks and valleys, such as a salary bonus or unexpected bills. While past events inform us, they don't bind us, and armed with insights into your income and expenditure over the last financial year, you are in a better position to move forward with your financial plans.

"The only way you will ever permanently take control of your financial life is to dig deep and fix the root problem."

—SUZE ORMAN—

Financial advisor and personal finance expert

Year in *review*

Taking a moment to review your financial health before planning the year ahead is essential. Learning from your past actions, both positive and negative, can help improve your money management skills for the future.

1 Start by reviewing your spending in the past 12 months. Where did your money go? Are you satisfied with your spending? Be honest and identify any regrets.

2 Consider your income. Did you stay within your means? Or did you exceed your income with your spending? If yes, how? If no, why?

3 Now let's calculate your net worth, which is the difference between what you own and what you owe. Use this number as a benchmark to measure your success 12 months from now.

DESCRIPTION	BALANCE
CASH *(This is your wallet, bank accounts, and any cash you have hidden away)*	
INVESTMENTS *(Things like stocks and retirement accounts)*	
PROPERTY *(Your home or any land you own)*	
BUSINESSES *(If you own a business, even a small one, it counts)*	
OTHER ASSETS *(Anything else that you could sell if you needed to, like a car)*	
TOTAL ASSETS	

DESCRIPTION	BALANCE
HOUSE DEBT *(If you borrowed money to buy your home, e.g., a mortgage)*	
LOANS *(Money you owe for college, a car, or anything else)*	
CREDIT CARD DEBT *(Any expenses you're paying off over time)*	
OTHER DEBTS *(Anything else you might owe)*	
TOTAL LIABILITIES	

MY NET WORTH:

What you own—What you owe

= $ ....

4 Write your motivation for the next 12 months.

....

....

....

....

Step 2: *Write down your money story*

Dive deeper into your personal money story by visualizing or writing out the highs and lows that you've experienced with your finances. Keep in mind that each person's financial journey is unique, and it is shaped by their upbringing, life decisions, and habits.

Our money habits in adulthood are not always easy to change, because they're formed early in life and often become a subconscious part of how we live our lives. Our parents are often our first teachers and also our most lasting examples of how to handle finances. If our earliest memories of money management involve seeing our parents struggle to make ends meet, it's likely to impact our own attitudes toward money as we grow up.

However, how you started does not have to be how you end. The first step toward change is reflecting on and understanding your own behavior around money.

Use these questions to dive deeper into the layers of your financial history and beliefs, to give you a valuable insight into your personal money story.

1 How would you characterize your parents' or guardians' approach to money? Did they struggle, save, invest, or spend frivolously?

2 Have you identified any deep-seated money habits or beliefs that you've carried from childhood? If so, what are they?

3 Can you recall a pivotal financial moment in your life that significantly changed your perspective on money?

4 How have your life decisions, both big and small, shaped your current financial situation?

5 In what ways do you believe your upbringing has influenced your current financial habits?

6 Have you ever tried to change a money habit that you realized was negatively impacting your financial health? How did you go about it?

"Define success on your own terms, achieve it by your own rules, and build a life you're proud to live."

—ANNE SWEENEY—

Entertainment executive and businesswoman

Step 3: *Envision your dream life*

When you have reflected on your past and come to understand your current finances, shift your gaze to the future. Envisioning your dream life is more than daydreaming—it's pivotal for impactful financial decisions.

Ask yourself: What's paramount in your life? Your answers—whether family, travel, or career—will unveil your core values.

Visualize this dream life in detail—where you live, where you work, and the relationships you value. From this, determine short-term goals, like specialized courses or travels, and long-term goals, like early retirement or a philanthropic legacy. Record these visions, as these will guide your financial journey.

Ask *yourself*

Use these questions to reflect on what kind of life you envision for yourself. Bear in mind, as life evolves so might your dreams. What is most important is to keep your financial decisions aligned with your evolving goals and values.

1   What are my top priorities in life, and how can my finances help me get there?

2   Thinking long term, where do I want to be financially in 10 years?

3   If I could achieve just one financial milestone in the next year, what would it be, and why?

Step 4: Set your financial goals

Imagine this; you aspire to achieve absolute financial freedom. You want to transform your dreams into tangible accomplishments, like being completely debt-free, being able to retire early, or being able to buy property.

A well-crafted action plan is what stands between you and your dreams, and it all starts with setting clear goals. Hitting a goal will ignite a blaze of possibilities, fueling your ambitions. You're in control of your financial dreams, and there's no "wrong time" to set new goals. As long as you're determined and disciplined, you're set for success.

"The biggest adventure you can take is to live the life of your dreams."

—OPRAH WINFREY—

The golden rules of
setting goals

Goals turn aspirations into focused targets, guiding your actions with purpose. By setting goals, you can track your progress. Checking off achieved goals boosts excitement and motivates you to accomplish more.

Do you know SMART goals, where Specific, Measurable, Achievable, Realistic, and Time-bound strategies fuel your journey to financial success? Now, let these principles be your guide in setting effective goals.

"I was taught that the way of progress was neither swift nor easy."

—MARIE CURIE—

BE **SPECIFIC**

Instead of vague goals like "save money," be specific. For example, break financial improvement into concrete actionable steps like "create a budget." For even more precision, specify saving $500 per month for the rest of the year under "create a budget."

ENSURE **MEASURABILITY**

To ensure clarity of progress, it is important to establish measurability. For instance, when planning for a vacation, set a specific goal of saving $1,000 in 8 months. Make this goal measurable by saving $125 every month.

MAKE IT **ACHIEVABLE**

Achieve breakthroughs by taking realistic steps. Avoid setting unrealistic expectations that can discourage you. If you have $5,000 in credit card debt, aim to pay off a feasible amount based on your current income. Resist the temptation of aiming for impractical leaps.

KEEP IT **REALISTIC**

Similarly, challenge yourself, but avoid setting impossible missions. For instance, if you have recently started a new job, it would be unrealistic to immediately ask for a huge raise. Be realistic and set goals that are challenging yet attainable.

TIME YOUR GOALS

Set deadlines for goals to promote focus and urgency. Tracking progress and setting time-sensitive targets will help you stay on track and ensure priorities align with desired outcomes. This will drive results and create a sense of accomplishment.

Setting *goals*

Write down your 5 financial goals for the coming year. Break them into monthly subgoals to help you track your progress month by month. Feel the commitment as you write—you're making a pact with yourself.

When in doubt, use these questions to guide your goal setting:

What is my goal and subgoal? How will I know when I achieve it? Is the goal realistic, and how will I accomplish it? Why is it important to me? What is my deadline?

Goal 1 ....

....

....

MONTHLY SUBGOAL ....

....

MY GOAL IS ...

Specific ☐

Measurable ☐

Achievable ☐

Realistic ☐

Time-bound ☐

Goal 2 ....

....

....

MONTHLY SUBGOAL ....

....

MY GOAL IS ...

Specific ☐

Measurable ☐

Achievable ☐

Realistic ☐

Time-bound ☐

Goal 3 ....

....

....

MONTHLY SUBGOAL ....

....

MY GOAL IS ...

Specific ☐

Measurable ☐

Achievable ☐

Realistic ☐

Time-bound ☐

Goal 4 ....

....

....

MONTHLY SUBGOAL ....

....

MY GOAL IS ...

Specific ☐

Measurable ☐

Achievable ☐

Realistic ☐

Time-bound ☐

Goal 5 ....

....

....

MONTHLY SUBGOAL ....

....

MY GOAL IS ...

Specific ☐

Measurable ☐

Achievable ☐

Realistic ☐

Time-bound ☐

Step 5: *Identify your financial habits*

Your journey to financial success is not just about numbers; it's about the daily habits that define it. Even small actions, like earning interest, can have a big impact. Our habits go beyond actions; they shape our identity and how we manage money.

It's important to understand that our actions are driven by triggers and reinforced by rewards. This dynamic, better known as the "habit loop," affects not only our finances but also other aspects of life, like impulse buying.

Building on the book *Atomic Habits* by James Clear, the four steps on the opposite page help us identify and understand the habits that greatly influence our financial decisions. By recognizing and adjusting these habits, we can align our finances with our values and goals, creating a strong foundation for our desired financial future.

Identifying your *habits*

By identifying your financial habits—the cues, cravings, responses, and rewards—you can steer your approach to money management to fulfill your dreams and aspirations.

1. CUE (TRIGGER)
Recognize what prompts your financial behaviors. Does stress lead to impulsive spending? Or perhaps a pay day triggers immediate indulgence?

2. CRAVING (DESIRE)
Understand the emotional response behind the cue. Do you spend to feel better, or save to feel secure?

3. RESPONSE (ROUTINE)
This is the actual habit. Maybe you buy coffee every morning as you walk past the cafe, or you save a bit of money after receiving a pay check.

4. REWARD
Identify the satisfaction you get from the habit. Is it the taste of coffee or the joy of watching your savings grow?

Identify *your habits*

If you've got some habits you'd like to change, you might have realized breaking them isn't quite as easy as you imagined. Now take the time to use the habit loop framework to identify and understand your habits.

---

1   Identify triggers that prompt your financial behaviors, then reflect on the emotional response behind each of them.

TRIGGER *(example)* .... WHEN I'M STRESSED, I OFTEN BUY EXPENSIVE TAKEOUT

EMOTIONAL RESPONSE *(example)* .... I'VE "EARNED" TAKEOUT; IT MAKES ME FEEL RELAXED

TRIGGER ....

EMOTIONAL RESPONSE ....

TRIGGER ....

EMOTIONAL RESPONSE ....

TRIGGER ....

EMOTIONAL RESPONSE ....

TRIGGER ....

EMOTIONAL RESPONSE ....

TRIGGER ....

EMOTIONAL RESPONSE ....

2 What current financial habits will you change and with what new financial habit? Remember, new habits should help guide you to achieve your goals.

OLD HABIT *(example)* ... I SPEND TOO MUCH MONEY ON EXPENSIVE TAKEOUT

NEW HABIT *(example)* ... I WANT TO COOK MORE OFTEN

OLD HABIT ....

NEW HABIT ....

OLD HABIT ....

NEW HABIT ....

OLD HABIT ....

NEW HABIT ....

OLD HABIT ....

NEW HABIT ....

OLD HABIT ....

NEW HABIT ....

3 Write down your motivation and how you will succeed with your new habits.

....

....

Step 6: Create your budget

Creating a budget is crucial for the year ahead. We believe this is the most important element in financial success, and for that reason, it takes longer than the previous five steps.

A budget helps you track your money and work toward your financial goals. It's not about restricting yourself from enjoying life but about understanding your finances and ensuring you spend as intended. Remember that budgets are flexible and can be adjusted as your financial situation changes.

We recommend following the 50/30/20 rule. Allocate 50% of your income for necessities, 30% for fun, and 20% for your security and future goals.

Note to the reader: Take a moment to evaluate your current financial situation, salary, age, and long-term goals. If these percentages seem difficult to achieve given your current income, start from where you are and gradually work toward the ideal percentages as your salary increases.

The 50/30/20 rule
explained

50% FOR NECESSITIES

Half of your after-tax income should be allocated to essential expenses such as housing and utilities. This will provide stability and comfort and create a solid foundation for your lifestyle.

30% FOR FUN!

Allocate a smaller portion of your budget for enjoyable experiences such as dining out and entertainment. This way, you can treat yourself without jeopardizing your financial goals.

20% FOR FUTURE YOU

This is for your financial future. It includes saving, paying off debt, and investing. Think long term, prioritize your F*** U Fund (see page 36), then focus on retirement and other financial goals.

How to allocate the 20% for future you:
1. Save 10–12% of your income until you have enough for 3–6 months of expenses or income. (Also take into account your F*** U Fund.)
2. Allocate 5–7% of your budget for investing. This is a great way to grow your money. The longer your time horizon is, the greater risk you can take.
3. For retirement, start with 3–5% of your budget and increase your contributions as you get closer to your retirement.

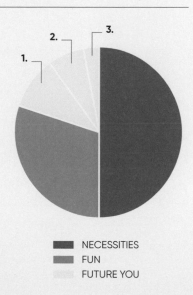

NECESSITIES
FUN
FUTURE YOU

Putting the 50/30/20 rule *into action*

STEP 1   Calculate the categories

Begin by calculating how much money should be allocated to necessities, fun, and future you.

EXAMPLE: Let's say your monthly income is $2,600 (after tax and retirement contributions). So your allocations could be:

$$\begin{aligned}
\textbf{NECESSITIES:} && \$2,600 \times 0.5 &= \$1,300 \\
\textbf{FUN:} && \$2,600 \times 0.3 &= \$780 \\
\textbf{FUTURE YOU:} && \$2,600 \times 0.2 &= \$520
\end{aligned}$$

CATEGORIES	YOUR SALARY (after tax & retirement)	ALLOCATION	TOTAL
Necessities	....	0.5	....
Fun	....	0.3	....
Future You	....	0.2	....

Notes: ....

....

....

....

....

....

STEP 2 · Categorize your spending habits

Categorize your spending habits using the 50/30/20 rule. If you're already spending more than 50% on necessities or more than 30% on fun, don't worry. Creating a budget takes effort, but try to follow the rule as closely as possible.

NECESSITIES	FUN	FUTURE YOU
(All nonnegotiable expenses)	*(All nice-to-have expenses)*	*(All your savings & financial goals)*
....	....	....
....	....	....
....	....	....
....	....	....
....	....	....
....	....	....
....	....	....
....	....	....
....	....	....
....	....	....
....	....	....
....	....	....
....	....	....
Total	*Total*	*Total* ....

Please note: If your total is higher than your total from step 1, it means that you will be spending more than you earn.

Additional things to consider

STEP 3   Automate your savings

A great way to save money is by setting up an automatic transfer from your main account to your savings and investment accounts shortly after pay day. This will help you build your savings without even thinking about it!

STEP 4   Monthly check-in

At the beginning of every month, check in on your budget to make sure you are progressing in the way you want to and that you are splitting your expenses between necessities, fun, and future you in a way that works for you and your current income.

F*** U Fund explained

Investing secures your financial aspirations for the future, but it's important to also consider your present needs. That's why having an emergency savings account is crucial. We call it the F*** U Fund. This fund is the cash you keep in your savings account, always within reach, and it's your ultimate safety net. It empowers you to make bold choices, like leaving a job or starting a new venture.

To start building your fund, aim to save enough to cover three to six months of expenses. If you are freelance, aim for six months' worth of average income. If you have a stable job and low expenses, three months' salary may be enough.

Building your F*** U Fund may feel challenging, but it's worth it. It can provide you with the freedom to make independent choices, sleep peacefully, and pursue a fulfilling life. It's time to take control of your finances and start building your safety net!

It's time to take control of your finances and start building your safety net.

Part 2

Track your progress: *charting monthly and weekly milestones*

To steer your success you need to plan, review, and reflect on your monthly and weekly progress. This part of the planner is designed to guide you through that process.

How to work through
the planner

The planner is divided into 12 months, providing tools to review, plan, and reflect on your finances on a weekly, monthly, and yearly basis that will help you effectively manage your money and achieve your financial goals.

At the start of every month, it's a good idea to keep a record of what you own (assets) and what you owe (liabilities). This will help you figure out your net worth, which is a great way to keep track of your financial health. Use the **Monthly Net Worth Tracker** to see how you're doing over time and spot any areas that might need some attention.

Then make a budget for the upcoming month. Use the **Monthly Planning Tool** to make sure you stay within your means. First, list your expected income. Then, divide your funds based on the 50/30/20 rule. Check that your planned expenses do not go over your income to maintain financial stability. Review this regularly during the month to stay in control of your monthly finances and make any necessary adjustments.

Use the **Monthly Habit Tracker** to keep track of and record your new habits. It's perfect for staying on top of your financial goals. For example, you can use this tool to monitor habits like saving a specific amount of money every week, cutting down on unnecessary expenses, or even increasing your income. See this tool as a motivation to develop positive financial habits.

Every week, turn to the **Weekly Calendar** to stay on top of the upcoming seven days. It's a great tool to plan your daily money tasks, such as paying bills, saving money, or working toward your financial goals. By being prepared for your weekly money responsibilities, you can avoid any unexpected surprises and stay organized.

Then, take some time to do a **Weekly Review**. Think about your financial successes, difficulties, and things you learned. Did you follow your budget? Were there any surprises with your expenses? Did you move closer to your financial goals? This review helps you learn from your experiences and make changes for the next week.

At the end of each month, it is time to reflect on your financial performance. Use the **Monthly Review** to gain a clearer picture of your biggest wins and challenges. See if there's anything you should consider stopping, starting, or continuing in the next month. Track the progress of your monthly subgoals and make adjustments to your financial plans, making sure you're moving closer to your long-term financial goals.

By consistently using these tools in the planner, you'll have everything you need to effectively manage your finances, make well-informed decisions, and work toward your financial goals. Remember, financial planning is an ongoing process, so it's important to regularly track and review your progress to achieve success.

"Trying to do it all and expecting that it all can be done exactly right is a recipe for disappointment. Perfection is the enemy."

—SHERYL SANDBERG—
Former Meta COO

Monthly *Net Worth Tracker*

Calculate your net worth at the start of a new month to track your financial health.

DATE OF REVIEW ....   **LAST MONTH'S NET WORTH** ....
(USE YOUR NET WORTH FROM PAGE 15)

What you own (assets)

First, gather everything you have:

DESCRIPTION	BALANCE
CASH *(This is your wallet, bank accounts, and any cash you have hidden away)*	
INVESTMENTS *(Things like stocks and retirement accounts)*	
PROPERTY *(Your home or any land you own)*	
BUSINESSES *(If you own a business, even a small one, it counts)*	
OTHER ASSETS *(Anything else that you could sell if you needed to, like a car)*	
TOTAL ASSETS	

What you owe (liabilities)

Now, let's look at what you owe:

DESCRIPTION	BALANCE
HOUSE DEBT *(If you borrowed money to buy your home, e.g., a mortgage)*	
LOANS *(Money you owe for college, a car, or anything else)*	
CREDIT CARD DEBT *(Any expenses you're paying off over time)*	
OTHER DEBTS *(Anything else you might owe)*	
TOTAL LIABILITIES	

MY NET WORTH:

What you own – What you owe

= $..

LAST MONTH VS. THIS MONTH

CHANGES IN $	THIS MONTH – LAST MONTH = $...
CHANGE IN PERCENTAGE (%)	CHANGE IN $ / LAST MONTH'S NET WORTH = ... %

Monthly *Planning*

Plan for the month ahead.
Set a reminder to do this on the first day of each month.

MONTH OF ....

SALARY

FIXED INCOME ....

VARIABLE INCOME
(BONUS, DIVIDENDS, SIDE HUSTLE, ETC.) ....

TOTAL INCOME ....

EXPENSES: NECESSITIES (Aim for 50% of your income)

Fill out the budget category at the beginning of the month with what you expect to spend, then fill out the actual category at the end of the month with what you ended up spending.

ITEM	BUDGET	ACTUAL
....	....	....
....	....	....
....	....	....
....	....	....
....	....	....
....	....	....

EXPENSES: FUN (Aim for 30% of your income)

Fill out the budget category at the beginning of the month with what you expect to spend, then fill out the actual category at the end of the month with what you ended up spending.

ITEM	BUDGET	ACTUAL
....	....	....
....	....	....
....	....	....
....	....	....
....	....	....
....	....	....

EXPENSES: FUTURE YOU (Aim for 20% of your income)

Fill out the budget category at the beginning of the month with what you expect to spend, then fill out the actual category at the end of the month with what you ended up spending.

ITEM	BUDGET	ACTUAL
....	....	....
....	....	....
....	....	....
....	....	....

Monthly *Habit Tracker*

*Use this tracker to track the new habits you defined on page
31. Mark the days on the calendar with the corresponding
number for each habit where you stuck to your new behavior.*

MONTH .... YEAR ....

LIST YOUR NEW HABITS HERE:

1 ....

2 ....

3 ....

4 ....

5 ....

Mon	*Tue*	*Wed*	*Thu*	*Fri*	*Sat*	*Sun*

Weekly *Calendar*

Use this calendar as a financial overview.
Start the week by adding special events and things
you need to consider in your budget this week.

MONTH .... YEAR ....

DATE	FINANCIAL MILESTONES, ACTIONS, AND DEADLINES
Mon	
Tue	
Wed	
Thu	
Fri	
Sat	
Sun	

Weekly *Review*

End each week with a review of how well you succeeded.

WEEK OF ....

CELEBRATE: Write down your wins of the past week (big or small)

1 ....

2 ....

3 ....

REFLECT: What could have gone better?

1 ....

2 ....

3 ....

LEARN: What has this taught you?

1 ....

2 ....

3 ....

WEEKLY REVIEW: How many stars do you give yourself?

☆ ☆ ☆
☆ ☆

RECOMMIT: Remind yourself of your big goal. Why are you doing this?

....

....

....

Weekly *Calendar*

MONTH .... YEAR ....

DATE	FINANCIAL MILESTONES, ACTIONS, AND DEADLINES
Mon	
Tue	
Wed	
Thu	
Fri	
Sat	
Sun	

Weekly *Review*

WEEK OF ....

CELEBRATE: Write down your wins of the past week (big or small)

1 ....

2 ....

3 ....

REFLECT: What could have gone better?

1 ....

2 ....

3 ....

LEARN: What has this taught you?

1 ....

2 ....

3 ....

WEEKLY REVIEW: How many stars do you give yourself?

☆ ☆ ☆
☆ ☆

RECOMMIT: Remind yourself of your big goal. Why are you doing this?

....

....

....

Weekly *Calendar*

MONTH .... YEAR ....

DATE	FINANCIAL MILESTONES, ACTIONS, AND DEADLINES
Mon	
Tue	
Wed	
Thu	
Fri	
Sat	
Sun	

Weekly *Review*

WEEK OF ....

CELEBRATE: Write down your wins of the past week (big or small)

1 ....

2 ....

3 ....

REFLECT: What could have gone better?

1 ....

2 ....

3 ....

LEARN: What has this taught you?

1 ....

2 ....

3 ....

WEEKLY REVIEW: How many stars do you give yourself?

☆ ☆ ☆
☆ ☆

RECOMMIT: Remind yourself of your big goal. Why are you doing this?

....

....

....

Weekly *Calendar*

MONTH .... YEAR ....

DATE	FINANCIAL MILESTONES, ACTIONS, AND DEADLINES
Mon	....
Tue	....
Wed	....
Thu	....
Fri	....
Sat	....
Sun	....

Weekly *Review*

WEEK OF ....

CELEBRATE: Write down your wins of the past week (big or small)

1 ....

2 ....

3 ....

REFLECT: What could have gone better?

1 ....

2 ....

3 ....

LEARN: What has this taught you?

1 ....

2 ....

3 ....

WEEKLY REVIEW: How many stars do you give yourself?

☆ ☆ ☆
☆ ☆

RECOMMIT: Remind yourself of your big goal. Why are you doing this?

....

....

....

Monthly *Review*

MONTH OF ....

Money Mood

○ ○ ○ ○ ○ ○ ○

☐   ☐   ☐
upset   neutral   excited

WHAT WENT WELL THIS MONTH?

THINGS TO DO

STOP DOING ....

START DOING ....

KEEP DOING ....

MY BIGGEST WINS

MY BIGGEST CHALLENGES

MONTHLY SUBGOAL TRACKER

0%   100%

1

2

3

4

5

OTHER REFLECTIONS

Monthly *Net Worth Tracker*

DATE OF REVIEW .... LAST MONTH'S NET WORTH ....

What you own (assets)

First, gather everything you have:

DESCRIPTION	BALANCE
CASH *(This is your wallet, bank accounts, and any cash you have hidden away)*	
INVESTMENTS *(Things like stocks and retirement accounts)*	
PROPERTY *(Your home or any land you own)*	
BUSINESSES *(If you own a business, even a small one, it counts)*	
OTHER ASSETS *(Anything else that you could sell if you needed to, like a car)*	
TOTAL ASSETS	

What you owe (liabilities)

Now, let's look at what you owe:

DESCRIPTION	BALANCE
HOUSE DEBT *(If you borrowed money to buy your home, e.g., a mortgage)*	
LOANS *(Money you owe for college, a car, or anything else)*	
CREDIT CARD DEBT *(Any expenses you're paying off over time)*	
OTHER DEBTS *(Anything else you might owe)*	
TOTAL LIABILITIES	

MY NET WORTH:

What you own – What you owe

= $..

LAST MONTH VS. THIS MONTH	
CHANGES IN $	THIS MONTH – LAST MONTH = $ ....
CHANGE IN PERCENTAGE (%)	CHANGE IN $ / LAST MONTH'S NET WORTH = ... %

Monthly *Planning*

MONTH OF ....

SALARY

FIXED INCOME ....

VARIABLE INCOME
(BONUS, DIVIDENDS, SIDE-HUSTLE, ETC.) ....

TOTAL INCOME ....

EXPENSES: NECESSITIES (Aim for 50% of your income)

Fill out the budget category at the beginning of the month with what you expect to spend, then fill out the actual category at the end of the month with what you ended up spending.

ITEM	BUDGET	ACTUAL
....	....	....
....	....	....
....	....	....
....	....	....
....	....	....
....	....	....

EXPENSES: FUN (Aim for 30% of your income)

Fill out the budget category at the beginning of the month with what you expect to spend, then fill out the actual category at the end of the month with what you ended up spending.

ITEM	BUDGET	ACTUAL
....	....	....
....	....	....
....	....	....
....	....	....
....	....	....
....	....	....

EXPENSES: FUTURE YOU (Aim for 20% of your income)

Fill out the budget category at the beginning of the month with what you expect to spend, then fill out the actual category at the end of the month with what you ended up spending.

ITEM	BUDGET	ACTUAL
....	....	....
....	....	....
....	....	....
....	....	....

Monthly *Habit Tracker*

MONTH .... YEAR ....

LIST YOUR NEW HABITS HERE:

1 ....

2 ....

3 ....

4 ....

5 ....

Mon	*Tue*	*Wed*	*Thu*	*Fri*	*Sat*	*Sun*

Weekly *Calendar*

MONTH .... YEAR ....

DATE	FINANCIAL MILESTONES, ACTIONS, AND DEADLINES
Mon	
Tue	
Wed	
Thu	
Fri	
Sat	
Sun	

Weekly *Review*

WEEK OF ....

CELEBRATE: Write down your wins of the past week (big or small)

1 ....

2 ....

3 ....

REFLECT: What could have gone better?

1 ....

2 ....

3 ....

LEARN: What has this taught you?

1 ....

2 ....

3 ....

WEEKLY REVIEW: How many stars do you give yourself?

☆ ☆ ☆
☆ ☆

RECOMMIT: Remind yourself of your big goal. Why are you doing this?

....

....

....

Weekly *Calendar*

MONTH .... YEAR ....

DATE	FINANCIAL MILESTONES, ACTIONS, AND DEADLINES
Mon	
Tue	
Wed	
Thu	
Fri	
Sat	
Sun	

Weekly *Review*

WEEK OF ....

CELEBRATE: Write down your wins of the past week (big or small)

1 ....

2 ....

3 ....

REFLECT: What could have gone better?

1 ....

2 ....

3 ....

LEARN: What has this taught you?

1 ....

2 ....

3 ....

WEEKLY REVIEW: How many stars do you give yourself?

☆ ☆ ☆
☆ ☆

RECOMMIT: Remind yourself of your big goal. Why are you doing this?

....

....

....

Weekly *Calendar*

MONTH .... YEAR ....

DATE	FINANCIAL MILESTONES, ACTIONS, AND DEADLINES
Mon	
Tue	
Wed	
Thu	
Fri	
Sat	
Sun	

Weekly *Review*

WEEK OF ....

CELEBRATE: Write down your wins of the past week (big or small)

1 ....

2 ....

3 ....

REFLECT: What could have gone better?

1 ....

2 ....

3 ....

LEARN: What has this taught you?

1 ....

2 ....

3 ....

WEEKLY REVIEW: How many stars do you give yourself?	**RECOMMIT:** Remind yourself of your big goal. Why are you doing this?
☆ ☆ ☆ ☆ ☆	....

Weekly *Calendar*

MONTH .... YEAR ....

DATE	FINANCIAL MILESTONES, ACTIONS, AND DEADLINES
Mon	
Tue	
Wed	
Thu	
Fri	
Sat	
Sun	

Weekly *Review*

WEEK OF ....

CELEBRATE: Write down your wins of the past week (big or small)

1 ....

2 ....

3 ....

REFLECT: What could have gone better?

1 ....

2 ....

3 ....

LEARN: What has this taught you?

1 ....

2 ....

3 ....

WEEKLY REVIEW: How many stars do you give yourself?

☆ ☆ ☆
☆ ☆

RECOMMIT: Remind yourself of your big goal. Why are you doing this?

....

....

....

Monthly *Review*

MONTH OF ....

Money Mood

( ) ( ) ( ) ( ) ( ) ( ) ( )

☐ upset   ☐ neutral   ☐ excited

WHAT WENT WELL THIS MONTH?

THINGS TO DO

STOP DOING ....

START DOING ....

KEEP DOING ....

MY BIGGEST WINS

MY BIGGEST CHALLENGES

MONTHLY SUBGOAL TRACKER

0%   100%

1

2

3

4

5

OTHER REFLECTIONS

Monthly *Net Worth Tracker*

DATE OF REVIEW .... **LAST MONTH'S NET WORTH** ....

What you own *(assets)*
First, gather everything you have:

DESCRIPTION	BALANCE
CASH *(This is your wallet, bank accounts, and any cash you have hidden away)*	
INVESTMENTS *(Things like stocks and retirement accounts)*	
PROPERTY *(Your home or any land you own)*	
BUSINESSES *(If you own a business, even a small one, it counts)*	
OTHER ASSETS *(Anything else that you could sell if you needed to, like a car)*	
TOTAL ASSETS	

What you owe *(liabilities)*
Now, let's look at what you owe:

DESCRIPTION	BALANCE
HOUSE DEBT *(If you borrowed money to buy your home, e.g., a mortgage)*	
LOANS *(Money you owe for college, a car, or anything else)*	
CREDIT CARD DEBT *(Any expenses you're paying off over time)*	
OTHER DEBTS *(Anything else you might owe)*	
TOTAL LIABILITIES	

MY NET WORTH:
What you own – What you owe

= $..

LAST MONTH VS. THIS MONTH	
CHANGES IN $	THIS MONTH – LAST MONTH = $ ....
CHANGE IN PERCENTAGE (%)	CHANGE IN $ / LAST MONTH'S NET WORTH = ... %

Monthly *Planning*

MONTH OF ....

SALARY

FIXED INCOME ....

VARIABLE INCOME ....
(BONUS, DIVIDENDS, SIDE HUSTLE, ETC.)

TOTAL INCOME ....

EXPENSES: NECESSITIES (Aim for 50% of your income)

Fill out the budget category at the beginning of the month with what you expect to spend, then fill out the actual category at the end of the month with what you ended up spending.

ITEM	BUDGET	ACTUAL
....	....	....
....	....	....
....	....	....
....	....	....
....	....	....
....	....	....

EXPENSES: FUN (Aim for 30% of your income)

Fill out the budget category at the beginning of the month with what you expect to spend, then fill out the actual category at the end of the month with what you ended up spending.

ITEM	BUDGET	ACTUAL

EXPENSES: FUTURE YOU (Aim for 20% of your income)

Fill out the budget category at the beginning of the month with what you expect to spend, then fill out the actual category at the end of the month with what you ended up spending.

ITEM	BUDGET	ACTUAL

MONTHLY AND WEEKLY REVIEW AND PLAN

Monthly *Habit Tracker*

MONTH .... YEAR ....

LIST YOUR NEW HABITS HERE:

1 ....

2 ....

3 ....

4 ....

5 ....

Mon	*Tue*	*Wed*	*Thu*	*Fri*	*Sat*	*Sun*

Weekly *Calendar*

MONTH .... **YEAR** ....

DATE	FINANCIAL MILESTONES, ACTIONS, AND DEADLINES
Mon	....
Tue	....
Wed	....
Thu	....
Fri	....
Sat	....
Sun	....

Weekly *Review*

WEEK OF ....

CELEBRATE: Write down your wins of the past week (big or small)

1 ....

2 ....

3 ....

REFLECT: What could have gone better?

1 ....

2 ....

3 ....

LEARN: What has this taught you?

1 ....

2 ....

3 ....

WEEKLY REVIEW: How many stars do you give yourself?

☆ ☆ ☆
☆ ☆

RECOMMIT: Remind yourself of your big goal. Why are you doing this?

....

....

....

Weekly *Calendar*

MONTH .... YEAR ....

DATE	FINANCIAL MILESTONES, ACTIONS, AND DEADLINES
Mon	
Tue	
Wed	
Thu	
Fri	
Sat	
Sun	

Weekly *Review*

WEEK OF ....

CELEBRATE: Write down your wins of the past week (big or small)

1 ....

2 ....

3 ....

REFLECT: What could have gone better?

1 ....

2 ....

3 ....

LEARN: What has this taught you?

1 ....

2 ....

3 ....

WEEKLY REVIEW: How many stars do you give yourself?

☆ ☆ ☆
☆ ☆

RECOMMIT: Remind yourself of your big goal. Why are you doing this?

....

....

....

Weekly *Calendar*

MONTH .... YEAR ....

DATE	FINANCIAL MILESTONES, ACTIONS, AND DEADLINES
Mon	
Tue	
Wed	
Thu	
Fri	
Sat	
Sun	

Weekly *Review*

CELEBRATE: Write down your wins of the past week (big or small)

1 ....

2 ....

3 ....

REFLECT: What could have gone better?

1 ....

2 ....

3 ....

LEARN: What has this taught you?

1 ....

2 ....

3 ....

WEEKLY REVIEW: How many stars do you give yourself?

☆ ☆ ☆
☆ ☆

RECOMMIT: Remind yourself of your big goal. Why are you doing this?

....

....

....

Weekly *Calendar*

MONTH .... YEAR ....

DATE	FINANCIAL MILESTONES, ACTIONS, AND DEADLINES
Mon	
Tue	
Wed	
Thu	
Fri	
Sat	
Sun	

Weekly *Review*

CELEBRATE: Write down your wins of the past week (big or small)

1 ....

2 ....

3 ....

REFLECT: What could have gone better?

1 ....

2 ....

3 ....

LEARN: What has this taught you?

1 ....

2 ....

3 ....

WEEKLY REVIEW: How many stars do you give yourself?

☆ ☆ ☆
☆ ☆

RECOMMIT: Remind yourself of your big goal. Why are you doing this?

....

....

....

Monthly *Review*

MONTH OF ....

Money Mood

○ ○ ○ ○ ○ ○ ○

☐   ☐   ☐

upset   neutral   excited

WHAT WENT WELL THIS MONTH?

THINGS TO DO

STOP DOING ....

START DOING ....

KEEP DOING ....

MY BIGGEST WINS

MY BIGGEST CHALLENGES

MONTHLY SUBGOAL TRACKER

0%   100%

1

2

3

4

5

OTHER REFLECTIONS

Monthly *Net Worth Tracker*

DATE OF REVIEW .... **LAST MONTH'S NET WORTH** ....

What you own (assets)

First, gather everything you have:

DESCRIPTION	BALANCE
CASH *(This is your wallet, bank accounts, and any cash you have hidden away)*	
INVESTMENTS *(Things like stocks and retirement accounts)*	
PROPERTY *(Your home or any land you own)*	
BUSINESSES *(If you own a business, even a small one, it counts)*	
OTHER ASSETS *(Anything else that you could sell if you needed to, like a car)*	
TOTAL ASSETS	

What you owe (liabilities)

Now, let's look at what you owe:

DESCRIPTION	BALANCE
HOUSE DEBT *(If you borrowed money to buy your home, e.g., a mortgage)*	
LOANS *(Money you owe for college, a car, or anything else)*	
CREDIT CARD DEBT *(Any expenses you're paying off over time)*	
OTHER DEBTS *(Anything else you might owe)*	
TOTAL LIABILITIES	

MY NET WORTH:

What you own – What you owe

= $ ....

LAST MONTH VS. THIS MONTH	
CHANGES IN $	THIS MONTH – LAST MONTH = $ ....
CHANGE IN PERCENTAGE (%)	CHANGE IN $ / LAST MONTH'S NET WORTH = ... %

Monthly *Planning*

MONTH OF ....

SALARY

FIXED INCOME ....

VARIABLE INCOME ....
(BONUS, DIVIDENDS, SIDE HUSTLE, ETC.)

TOTAL INCOME ....

EXPENSES: NECESSITIES (Aim for 50% of your income)

Fill out the budget category at the beginning of the month with what you expect to spend, then fill out the actual category at the end of the month with what you ended up spending.

ITEM	BUDGET	ACTUAL
....	....	....
....	....	....
....	....	....
....	....	....
....	....	....
....	....	....

EXPENSES: FUN (Aim for 30% of your income)

Fill out the budget category at the beginning of the month with what you expect to spend, then fill out the actual category at the end of the month with what you ended up spending.

ITEM	BUDGET	ACTUAL

EXPENSES: FUTURE YOU (Aim for 20% of your income)

Fill out the budget category at the beginning of the month with what you expect to spend, then fill out the actual category at the end of the month with what you ended up spending.

ITEM	BUDGET	ACTUAL

Monthly *Habit Tracker*

MONTH .... **YEAR** ....

LIST YOUR NEW HABITS HERE:

1 ....

2 ....

3 ....

4 ....

5 ....

Mon	*Tue*	*Wed*	*Thu*	*Fri*	*Sat*	*Sun*

Weekly *Calendar*

MONTH .... YEAR ....

DATE	FINANCIAL MILESTONES, ACTIONS, AND DEADLINES
Mon	
Tue	
Wed	
Thu	
Fri	
Sat	
Sun	

Weekly *Review*

WEEK OF ....

CELEBRATE: Write down your wins of the past week (big or small)

1 ....

2 ....

3 ....

REFLECT: What could have gone better?

1 ....

2 ....

3 ....

LEARN: What has this taught you?

1 ....

2 ....

3 ....

WEEKLY REVIEW: How many stars do you give yourself?	**RECOMMIT:** Remind yourself of your big goal. Why are you doing this?
☆ ☆ ☆ ☆ ☆	....

Weekly *Calendar*

MONTH ....   YEAR ....

DATE	FINANCIAL MILESTONES, ACTIONS, AND DEADLINES
Mon	
Tue	
Wed	
Thu	
Fri	
Sat	
Sun	

Weekly *Review*

WEEK OF ....

CELEBRATE: Write down your wins of the past week (big or small)

1 ....

2 ....

3 ....

REFLECT: What could have gone better?

1 ....

2 ....

3 ....

LEARN: What has this taught you?

1 ....

2 ....

3 ....

WEEKLY REVIEW: How many stars do you give yourself?

☆ ☆ ☆
☆ ☆

RECOMMIT: Remind yourself of your big goal. Why are you doing this?

....

....

....

Weekly *Calendar*

MONTH .... YEAR ....

DATE	FINANCIAL MILESTONES, ACTIONS, AND DEADLINES
Mon	
Tue	
Wed	
Thu	
Fri	
Sat	
Sun	

Weekly *Review*

WEEK OF ....

CELEBRATE: Write down your wins of the past week (big or small)

1 ....

2 ....

3 ....

REFLECT: What could have gone better?

1 ....

2 ....

3 ....

LEARN: What has this taught you?

1 ....

2 ....

3 ....

WEEKLY REVIEW: How many stars do you give yourself?

☆ ☆ ☆
☆ ☆

RECOMMIT: Remind yourself of your big goal. Why are you doing this?

....

....

....

Weekly *Calendar*

MONTH .... YEAR ....

DATE	FINANCIAL MILESTONES, ACTIONS, AND DEADLINES
Mon	
Tue	
Wed	
Thu	
Fri	
Sat	
Sun	

Weekly *Review*

WEEK OF ....

CELEBRATE: Write down your wins of the past week (big or small)

1 ....

2 ....

3 ....

REFLECT: What could have gone better?

1 ....

2 ....

3 ....

LEARN: What has this taught you?

1 ....

2 ....

3 ....

WEEKLY REVIEW: How many stars do you give yourself?

☆ ☆ ☆
☆ ☆

RECOMMIT: Remind yourself of your big goal. Why are you doing this?

....

....

....

Monthly *Review*

MONTH OF ....

Money Mood

⬤ ⬤ ⬤ ⬤ ⬤ ⬤ ⬤

☐   ☐   ☐
upset   neutral   excited

WHAT WENT WELL THIS MONTH?

....

....

....

....

THINGS TO DO

STOP DOING ....

....

START DOING ....

....

KEEP DOING ....

....

MY BIGGEST WINS

MY BIGGEST CHALLENGES

MONTHLY SUBGOAL TRACKER

0%   100%

1

2

3

4

5

OTHER REFLECTIONS

Monthly *Net Worth Tracker*

DATE OF REVIEW .... **LAST MONTH'S NET WORTH** ....

What you own (assets)

First, gather everything you have:

DESCRIPTION	BALANCE
CASH *(This is your wallet, bank accounts, and any cash you have hidden away)*	
INVESTMENTS *(Things like stocks and retirement accounts)*	
PROPERTY *(Your home or any land you own)*	
BUSINESSES *(If you own a business, even a small one, it counts)*	
OTHER ASSETS *(Anything else that you could sell if you needed to, like a car)*	
TOTAL ASSETS	

What you owe (liabilities)

Now, let's look at what you owe:

DESCRIPTION	BALANCE
HOUSE DEBT *(If you borrowed money to buy your home, e.g., a mortgage)*	
LOANS *(Money you owe for college, a car, or anything else)*	
CREDIT CARD DEBT *(Any expenses you're paying off over time)*	
OTHER DEBTS *(Anything else you might owe)*	
TOTAL LIABILITIES	

MY NET WORTH:

What you own – What you owe

= $ ....

LAST MONTH VS. THIS MONTH	
CHANGES IN $	THIS MONTH – LAST MONTH = $ ....
CHANGE IN PERCENTAGE (%)	CHANGE IN $ / LAST MONTH'S NET WORTH = ... %

Monthly *Planning*

MONTH OF ....

SALARY

FIXED INCOME ....

VARIABLE INCOME ....
(BONUS, DIVIDENDS, SIDE HUSTLE, ETC.)

TOTAL INCOME ....

EXPENSES: NECESSITIES (Aim for 50% of your income)

Fill out the budget category at the beginning of the month with what you expect to spend, then fill out the actual category at the end of the month with what you ended up spending.

ITEM	BUDGET	ACTUAL
....	....	....
....	....	....
....	....	....
....	....	....
....	....	....
....	....	....

EXPENSES: FUN (Aim for 30% of your income)

Fill out the budget category at the beginning of the month with what you expect to spend, then fill out the actual category at the end of the month with what you ended up spending.

ITEM	BUDGET	ACTUAL

EXPENSES: FUTURE YOU (Aim for 20% of your income)

Fill out the budget category at the beginning of the month with what you expect to spend, then fill out the actual category at the end of the month with what you ended up spending.

ITEM	BUDGET	ACTUAL

Monthly *Habit Tracker*

MONTH .... YEAR ....

LIST YOUR NEW HABITS HERE:

1 ....

2 ....

3 ....

4 ....

5 ....

Mon	Tue	Wed	Thu	Fri	Sat	Sun

Weekly *Calendar*

MONTH .... YEAR ....

DATE	FINANCIAL MILESTONES, ACTIONS, AND DEADLINES
Mon	....
Tue	....
Wed	....
Thu	....
Fri	....
Sat	....
Sun	....

Weekly *Review*

WEEK OF ....

CELEBRATE: Write down your wins of the past week (big or small)

1 ....

2 ....

3 ....

REFLECT: What could have gone better?

1 ....

2 ....

3 ....

LEARN: What has this taught you?

1 ....

2 ....

3 ....

WEEKLY REVIEW: How many stars do you give yourself?

☆ ☆ ☆
☆ ☆

RECOMMIT: Remind yourself of your big goal. Why are you doing this?

....

....

....

Weekly *Calendar*

MONTH .... YEAR ....

DATE	FINANCIAL MILESTONES, ACTIONS, AND DEADLINES
Mon	
Tue	
Wed	
Thu	
Fri	
Sat	
Sun	

Weekly *Review*

WEEK OF ....

CELEBRATE: Write down your wins of the past week (big or small)

1 ....

2 ....

3 ....

REFLECT: What could have gone better?

1 ....

2 ....

3 ....

LEARN: What has this taught you?

1 ....

2 ....

3 ....

WEEKLY REVIEW: How many stars do you give yourself?

☆ ☆ ☆
☆ ☆

RECOMMIT: Remind yourself of your big goal. Why are you doing this?

....

....

....

Weekly *Calendar*

MONTH .... YEAR ....

DATE	FINANCIAL MILESTONES, ACTIONS, AND DEADLINES
Mon	....
Tue	....
Wed	....
Thu	....
Fri	....
Sat	....
Sun	....

Weekly *Review*

WEEK OF ....

CELEBRATE: Write down your wins of the past week (big or small)

1 ....

2 ....

3 ....

REFLECT: What could have gone better?

1 ....

2 ....

3 ....

LEARN: What has this taught you?

1 ....

2 ....

3 ....

WEEKLY REVIEW: How many stars do you give yourself?

☆ ☆ ☆
☆ ☆

RECOMMIT: Remind yourself of your big goal. Why are you doing this?

....

....

....

Weekly *Calendar*

MONTH .... YEAR ....

DATE	FINANCIAL MILESTONES, ACTIONS, AND DEADLINES
Mon	
Tue	
Wed	
Thu	
Fri	
Sat	
Sun	

Weekly *Review*

WEEK OF ....

CELEBRATE: Write down your wins of the past week (big or small)

1 ....

2 ....

3 ....

REFLECT: What could have gone better?

1 ....

2 ....

3 ....

LEARN: What has this taught you?

1 ....

2 ....

3 ....

WEEKLY REVIEW: How many stars do you give yourself?

☆ ☆ ☆
☆ ☆

RECOMMIT: Remind yourself of your big goal. Why are you doing this?

....

....

....

Monthly *Review*

MONTH OF ....

Money Mood

○ ○ ○ ○ ○ ○ ○

☐   ☐   ☐
upset   neutral   excited

WHAT WENT WELL THIS MONTH?

....

....

....

....

THINGS TO DO

STOP DOING ....

....

START DOING ....

....

KEEP DOING ....

....

MY BIGGEST WINS

....

....

MY BIGGEST CHALLENGES

....

....

MONTHLY SUBGOAL TRACKER

0%   100%

1

2

3

4

5

OTHER REFLECTIONS

....

....

Monthly *Net Worth Tracker*

DATE OF REVIEW .... **LAST MONTH'S NET WORTH** ....

What you own (assets)
First, gather everything you have:

DESCRIPTION	BALANCE
CASH *(This is your wallet, bank accounts, and any cash you have hidden away)*	
INVESTMENTS *(Things like stocks and retirement accounts)*	
PROPERTY *(Your home or any land you own)*	
BUSINESSES *(If you own a business, even a small one, it counts)*	
OTHER ASSETS *(Anything else that you could sell if you needed to, like a car)*	
TOTAL ASSETS	

What you owe (liabilities)
Now, let's look at what you owe:

DESCRIPTION	BALANCE
HOUSE DEBT *(If you borrowed money to buy your home, e.g., a mortgage)*	
LOANS *(Money you owe for college, a car, or anything else)*	
CREDIT CARD DEBT *(Any expenses you're paying off over time)*	
OTHER DEBTS *(Anything else you might owe)*	
TOTAL LIABILITIES	

MY NET WORTH:
What you own – What you owe

= $ ....

LAST MONTH VS. THIS MONTH	
CHANGES IN $	THIS MONTH – LAST MONTH = $ ....
CHANGE IN PERCENTAGE (%)	CHANGE IN $ / LAST MONTH'S NET WORTH = ... %

Monthly *Planning*

MONTH OF ....

SALARY

FIXED INCOME ....

VARIABLE INCOME
(BONUS, DIVIDENDS, SIDE HUSTLE, ETC.) ....

TOTAL INCOME ....

EXPENSES: NECESSITIES (Aim for 50% of your income)

Fill out the budget category at the beginning of the month with what you expect to spend, then fill out the actual category at the end of the month with what you ended up spending.

ITEM	BUDGET	ACTUAL
....	....	....
....	....	....
....	....	....
....	....	....
....	....	....
....	....	....

EXPENSES: FUN (Aim for 30% of your income)

Fill out the budget category at the beginning of the month with what you expect to spend, then fill out the actual category at the end of the month with what you ended up spending.

ITEM	BUDGET	ACTUAL
....	....	....
....	....	....
....	....	....
....	....	....
....	....	....
....	....	....

EXPENSES: FUTURE YOU (Aim for 20% of your income)

Fill out the budget category at the beginning of the month with what you expect to spend, then fill out the actual category at the end of the month with what you ended up spending.

ITEM	BUDGET	ACTUAL
....	....	....
....	....	....
....	....	....
....	....	....

Monthly *Habit Tracker*

MONTH .... **YEAR** ....

LIST YOUR NEW HABITS HERE:

1 ....

2 ....

3 ....

4 ....

5 ....

Mon	*Tue*	*Wed*	*Thu*	*Fri*	*Sat*	*Sun*

Weekly *Calendar*

MONTH .... YEAR ....

DATE	FINANCIAL MILESTONES, ACTIONS, AND DEADLINES
Mon	
Tue	
Wed	
Thu	
Fri	
Sat	
Sun	

Weekly *Review*

WEEK OF ....

CELEBRATE: Write down your wins of the past week (big or small)

1 ....

2 ....

3 ....

REFLECT: What could have gone better?

1 ....

2 ....

3 ....

LEARN: What has this taught you?

1 ....

2 ....

3 ....

WEEKLY REVIEW: How many stars do you give yourself?

☆ ☆ ☆
☆ ☆

RECOMMIT: Remind yourself of your big goal. Why are you doing this?

....

....

....

Weekly *Calendar*

MONTH .... YEAR ....

DATE	FINANCIAL MILESTONES, ACTIONS, AND DEADLINES
Mon	
Tue	
Wed	
Thu	
Fri	
Sat	
Sun	

Weekly *Review*

WEEK OF ....

CELEBRATE: Write down your wins of the past week (big or small)

1 ....

2 ....

3 ....

REFLECT: What could have gone better?

1 ....

2 ....

3 ....

LEARN: What has this taught you?

1 ....

2 ....

3 ....

WEEKLY REVIEW: How many stars do you give yourself?

☆ ☆ ☆
☆ ☆

RECOMMIT: Remind yourself of your big goal. Why are you doing this?

....

....

....

Weekly *Calendar*

MONTH .... YEAR ....

DATE	FINANCIAL MILESTONES, ACTIONS, AND DEADLINES
Mon	
Tue	
Wed	
Thu	
Fri	
Sat	
Sun	

Weekly *Review*

WEEK OF ....

CELEBRATE: Write down your wins of the past week (big or small)

1 ....

2 ....

3 ....

REFLECT: What could have gone better?

1 ....

2 ....

3 ....

LEARN: What has this taught you?

1 ....

2 ....

3 ....

WEEKLY REVIEW: How many stars do you give yourself?

☆ ☆ ☆
☆ ☆

RECOMMIT: Remind yourself of your big goal. Why are you doing this?

....

....

....

Weekly *Calendar*

MONTH .... YEAR ....

DATE	FINANCIAL MILESTONES, ACTIONS, AND DEADLINES
Mon	
Tue	
Wed	
Thu	
Fri	
Sat	
Sun	

Weekly *Review*

WEEK OF ....

CELEBRATE: Write down your wins of the past week (big or small)

1 ....

2 ....

3 ....

REFLECT: What could have gone better?

1 ....

2 ....

3 ....

LEARN: What has this taught you?

1 ....

2 ....

3 ....

WEEKLY REVIEW: How many stars do you give yourself?

☆ ☆ ☆
☆ ☆

RECOMMIT: Remind yourself of your big goal. Why are you doing this?

....

....

....

Monthly *Review*

MONTH OF ....

Money Mood

☐ upset   ☐ neutral   ☐ excited

WHAT WENT WELL THIS MONTH?

....

....

....

....

THINGS TO DO

STOP DOING ....

....

START DOING ....

....

KEEP DOING ....

....

MY BIGGEST WINS

MY BIGGEST CHALLENGES

MONTHLY SUBGOAL TRACKER

0%   100%

1

2

3

4

5

OTHER REFLECTIONS

Monthly *Net Worth Tracker*

DATE OF REVIEW .... **LAST MONTH'S NET WORTH** ....

What you own (assets)

First, gather everything you have:

DESCRIPTION	BALANCE
CASH *(This is your wallet, bank accounts, and any cash you have hidden away)*	
INVESTMENTS *(Things like stocks and retirement accounts)*	
PROPERTY *(Your home or any land you own)*	
BUSINESSES *(If you own a business, even a small one, it counts)*	
OTHER ASSETS *(Anything else that you could sell if you needed to, like a car)*	
TOTAL ASSETS	

What you owe (liabilities)

Now, let's look at what you owe:

DESCRIPTION	BALANCE
HOUSE DEBT *(If you borrowed money to buy your home, e.g., a mortgage)*	
LOANS *(Money you owe for college, a car, or anything else)*	
CREDIT CARD DEBT *(Any expenses you're paying off over time)*	
OTHER DEBTS *(Anything else you might owe)*	
TOTAL LIABILITIES	

MY NET WORTH:

What you own – What you owe

= $..

LAST MONTH VS. THIS MONTH

CHANGES IN $	THIS MONTH – LAST MONTH = $ ....
CHANGE IN PERCENTAGE (%)	CHANGE IN $ / LAST MONTH'S NET WORTH = ... %

Monthly *Planning*

MONTH OF ....

SALARY

FIXED INCOME ....

VARIABLE INCOME
(BONUS, DIVIDENDS, SIDE HUSTLE, ETC.) ....

TOTAL INCOME ....

EXPENSES: NECESSITIES (Aim for 50% of your income)

Fill out the budget category at the beginning of the month with what you expect to spend, then fill out the actual category at the end of the month with what you ended up spending.

ITEM	BUDGET	ACTUAL
....	....	....
....	....	....
....	....	....
....	....	....
....	....	....
....	....	....

EXPENSES: FUN (Aim for 30% of your income)

Fill out the budget category at the beginning of the month with what you expect to spend, then fill out the actual category at the end of the month with what you ended up spending.

ITEM	BUDGET	ACTUAL

EXPENSES: FUTURE YOU (Aim for 20% of your income)

Fill out the budget category at the beginning of the month with what you expect to spend, then fill out the actual category at the end of the month with what you ended up spending.

ITEM	BUDGET	ACTUAL

Monthly *Habit Tracker*

MONTH .... YEAR ....

LIST YOUR NEW HABITS HERE:

1 ....

2 ....

3 ....

4 ....

5 ....

Mon	*Tue*	*Wed*	*Thu*	*Fri*	*Sat*	*Sun*

Weekly *Calendar*

MONTH .... **YEAR** ....

DATE	FINANCIAL MILESTONES, ACTIONS, AND DEADLINES
Mon	
Tue	
Wed	
Thu	
Fri	
Sat	
Sun	

Weekly *Review*

WEEK OF ....

CELEBRATE: Write down your wins of the past week (big or small)

1 ....

2 ....

3 ....

REFLECT: What could have gone better?

1 ....

2 ....

3 ....

LEARN: What has this taught you?

1 ....

2 ....

3 ....

WEEKLY REVIEW: How many stars do you give yourself?

☆ ☆ ☆
☆ ☆

RECOMMIT: Remind yourself of your big goal. Why are you doing this?

....

....

....

Weekly *Calendar*

MONTH .... YEAR ....

DATE	FINANCIAL MILESTONES, ACTIONS, AND DEADLINES
Mon	
Tue	
Wed	
Thu	
Fri	
Sat	
Sun	

Weekly *Review*

WEEK OF ....

CELEBRATE: Write down your wins of the past week (big or small)

1 ....

2 ....

3 ....

REFLECT: What could have gone better?

1 ....

2 ....

3 ....

LEARN: What has this taught you?

1 ....

2 ....

3 ....

WEEKLY REVIEW: How many stars do you give yourself?

☆ ☆ ☆
☆ ☆

RECOMMIT: Remind yourself of your big goal. Why are you doing this?

....

....

....

Weekly *Calendar*

MONTH .... YEAR ....

DATE	FINANCIAL MILESTONES, ACTIONS, AND DEADLINES
Mon	
Tue	
Wed	
Thu	
Fri	
Sat	
Sun	

Weekly *Review*

WEEK OF ....

CELEBRATE: Write down your wins of the past week (big or small)

1 ....

2 ....

3 ....

REFLECT: What could have gone better?

1 ....

2 ....

3 ....

LEARN: What has this taught you?

1 ....

2 ....

3 ....

WEEKLY REVIEW: How many stars do you give yourself?

☆ ☆ ☆
☆ ☆

RECOMMIT: Remind yourself of your big goal. Why are you doing this?

....

....

....

Weekly *Calendar*

MONTH .... YEAR ....

DATE	FINANCIAL MILESTONES, ACTIONS, AND DEADLINES
Mon	
Tue	
Wed	
Thu	
Fri	
Sat	
Sun	

Weekly *Review*

WEEK OF ....

CELEBRATE: Write down your wins of the past week (big or small)

1 ....

2 ....

3 ....

REFLECT: What could have gone better?

1 ....

2 ....

3 ....

LEARN: What has this taught you?

1 ....

2 ....

3 ....

WEEKLY REVIEW: How many stars do you give yourself?

☆ ☆ ☆
☆ ☆

RECOMMIT: Remind yourself of your big goal. Why are you doing this?

....

....

....

Monthly *Review*

MONTH OF ....

Money Mood

☐ upset   ☐ neutral   ☐ excited

WHAT WENT WELL THIS MONTH?

....

....

....

....

THINGS TO DO

STOP DOING ....

....

START DOING ....

....

KEEP DOING ....

....

MY BIGGEST WINS

MY BIGGEST CHALLENGES

MONTHLY SUBGOAL TRACKER

0%   100%

1

2

3

4

5

OTHER REFLECTIONS

Monthly *Net Worth Tracker*

DATE OF REVIEW .... **LAST MONTH'S NET WORTH** ....

What you own (assets)
First, gather everything you have:

DESCRIPTION	BALANCE
CASH *(This is your wallet, bank accounts, and any cash you have hidden away)*	
INVESTMENTS *(Things like stocks and retirement accounts)*	
PROPERTY *(Your home or any land you own)*	
BUSINESSES *(If you own a business, even a small one, it counts)*	
OTHER ASSETS *(Anything else that you could sell if you needed to, like a car)*	
TOTAL ASSETS	

What you owe (liabilities)
Now, let's look at what you owe:

DESCRIPTION	BALANCE
HOUSE DEBT *(If you borrowed money to buy your home, e.g., a mortgage)*	
LOANS *(Money you owe for college, a car, or anything else)*	
CREDIT CARD DEBT *(Any expenses you're paying off over time)*	
OTHER DEBTS *(Anything else you might owe)*	
TOTAL LIABILITIES	

MY NET WORTH:
What you own – What you owe

= $...

LAST MONTH VS. THIS MONTH

CHANGES IN $	THIS MONTH – LAST MONTH = $ ....
CHANGE IN PERCENTAGE (%)	CHANGE IN $ / LAST MONTH'S NET WORTH = ... %

Monthly *Planning*

MONTH OF ....

SALARY

FIXED INCOME ....

VARIABLE INCOME
(BONUS, DIVIDENDS, SIDE HUSTLE, ETC.) ....

TOTAL INCOME ....

EXPENSES: NECESSITIES (Aim for 50% of your income)

Fill out the budget category at the beginning of the month with what you expect to spend, then fill out the actual category at the end of the month with what you ended up spending.

ITEM	BUDGET	ACTUAL
....	....	....
....	....	....
....	....	....
....	....	....
....	....	....
....	....	....

EXPENSES: FUN (Aim for 30% of your income)

Fill out the budget category at the beginning of the month with what you expect to spend, then fill out the actual category at the end of the month with what you ended up spending.

ITEM	BUDGET	ACTUAL

EXPENSES: FUTURE YOU (Aim for 20% of your income)

Fill out the budget category at the beginning of the month with what you expect to spend, then fill out the actual category at the end of the month with what you ended up spending.

ITEM	BUDGET	ACTUAL

Monthly *Habit Tracker*

MONTH .... **YEAR** ....

LIST YOUR NEW HABITS HERE:

1 ....

2 ....

3 ....

4 ....

5 ....

Mon	*Tue*	*Wed*	*Thu*	*Fri*	*Sat*	*Sun*

Weekly *Calendar*

MONTH ....   YEAR ....

DATE	FINANCIAL MILESTONES, ACTIONS, AND DEADLINES
Mon	....
Tue	....
Wed	....
Thu	....
Fri	....
Sat	....
Sun	....

Weekly *Review*

WEEK OF ....

CELEBRATE: Write down your wins of the past week (big or small)

1 ....

2 ....

3 ....

REFLECT: What could have gone better?

1 ....

2 ....

3 ....

LEARN: What has this taught you?

1 ....

2 ....

3 ....

WEEKLY REVIEW: How many stars do you give yourself?

☆ ☆ ☆
☆ ☆

RECOMMIT: Remind yourself of your big goal. Why are you doing this?

....

....

....

Weekly *Calendar*

MONTH .... YEAR ....

DATE	FINANCIAL MILESTONES, ACTIONS, AND DEADLINES
Mon	
Tue	
Wed	
Thu	
Fri	
Sat	
Sun	

Weekly *Review*

WEEK OF ....

CELEBRATE: Write down your wins of the past week (big or small)

1 ....

2 ....

3 ....

REFLECT: What could have gone better?

1 ....

2 ....

3 ....

LEARN: What has this taught you?

1 ....

2 ....

3 ....

WEEKLY REVIEW: How many stars do you give yourself?

☆ ☆ ☆
☆ ☆

RECOMMIT: Remind yourself of your big goal. Why are you doing this?

....

....

....

Weekly *Calendar*

MONTH .... YEAR ....

DATE	FINANCIAL MILESTONES, ACTIONS, AND DEADLINES
Mon	
Tue	
Wed	
Thu	
Fri	
Sat	
Sun	

Weekly *Review*

WEEK OF ....

CELEBRATE: Write down your wins of the past week (big or small)

1 ....

2 ....

3 ....

REFLECT: What could have gone better?

1 ....

2 ....

3 ....

LEARN: What has this taught you?

1 ....

2 ....

3 ....

WEEKLY REVIEW: How many stars do you give yourself?

☆ ☆ ☆
☆ ☆

RECOMMIT: Remind yourself of your big goal. Why are you doing this?

....

....

....

Weekly *Calendar*

MONTH .... YEAR ....

DATE	FINANCIAL MILESTONES, ACTIONS, AND DEADLINES
Mon	
Tue	
Wed	
Thu	
Fri	
Sat	
Sun	

Weekly *Review*

WEEK OF ....

CELEBRATE: Write down your wins of the past week (big or small)

1 ....

2 ....

3 ....

REFLECT: What could have gone better?

1 ....

2 ....

3 ....

LEARN: What has this taught you?

1 ....

2 ....

3 ....

WEEKLY REVIEW: How many stars do you give yourself?

☆ ☆ ☆
☆ ☆

RECOMMIT: Remind yourself of your big goal. Why are you doing this?

....

....

....

Monthly *Review*

MONTH OF ....

Money Mood

○ ○ ○ ○ ○ ○ ○

☐   ☐   ☐
upset   neutral   excited

WHAT WENT WELL THIS MONTH?

....

....

....

....

THINGS TO DO

STOP DOING ....

....

START DOING ....

....

KEEP DOING ....

....

MY BIGGEST WINS

....

....

MY BIGGEST CHALLENGES

....

....

MONTHLY SUBGOAL TRACKER

0%   100%

1 ⬭

2 ⬭

3 ⬭

4 ⬭

5 ⬭

OTHER REFLECTIONS

....

....

Monthly *Net Worth Tracker*

DATE OF REVIEW .... **LAST MONTH'S NET WORTH** ....

What you own (assets)

First, gather everything you have:

DESCRIPTION	BALANCE
CASH *(This is your wallet, bank accounts, and any cash you have hidden away)*	
INVESTMENTS *(Things like stocks and retirement accounts)*	
PROPERTY *(Your home or any land you own)*	
BUSINESSES *(If you own a business, even a small one, it counts)*	
OTHER ASSETS *(Anything else that you could sell if you needed to, like a car)*	
TOTAL ASSETS	

What you owe (liabilities)

Now, let's look at what you owe:

DESCRIPTION	BALANCE
HOUSE DEBT *(If you borrowed money to buy your home, e.g., a mortgage)*	
LOANS *(Money you owe for college, a car, or anything else)*	
CREDIT CARD DEBT *(Any expenses you're paying off over time)*	
OTHER DEBTS *(Anything else you might owe)*	
TOTAL LIABILITIES	

MY NET WORTH:

What you own – What you owe

= $ ....

LAST MONTH VS. THIS MONTH	
CHANGES IN $	THIS MONTH – LAST MONTH = $ ....
CHANGE IN PERCENTAGE (%)	CHANGE IN $ / LAST MONTH'S NET WORTH = ... %

Monthly *Planning*

MONTH OF ....

SALARY

FIXED INCOME ....

VARIABLE INCOME ....
(BONUS, DIVIDENDS, SIDE HUSTLE, ETC.)

TOTAL INCOME ....

EXPENSES: NECESSITIES (Aim for 50% of your income)

Fill out the budget category at the beginning of the month with what you expect to spend, then fill out the actual category at the end of the month with what you ended up spending.

ITEM	BUDGET	ACTUAL
....	....	....
....	....	....
....	....	....
....	....	....
....	....	....
....	....	....

EXPENSES: FUN (Aim for 30% of your income)

Fill out the budget category at the beginning of the month with what you expect to spend, then fill out the actual category at the end of the month with what you ended up spending.

ITEM	BUDGET	ACTUAL
....	....	....
....	....	....
....	....	....
....	....	....
....	....	....
....	....	....

EXPENSES: FUTURE YOU (Aim for 20% of your income)

Fill out the budget category at the beginning of the month with what you expect to spend, then fill out the actual category at the end of the month with what you ended up spending.

ITEM	BUDGET	ACTUAL
....	....	....
....	....	....
....	....	....
....	....	....

Monthly *Habit Tracker*

MONTH .... YEAR ....

LIST YOUR NEW HABITS HERE:

1 ....

2 ....

3 ....

4 ....

5 ....

Mon	*Tue*	*Wed*	*Thu*	*Fri*	*Sat*	*Sun*

Weekly *Calendar*

MONTH .... YEAR ....

DATE	FINANCIAL MILESTONES, ACTIONS, AND DEADLINES
Mon	
Tue	
Wed	
Thu	
Fri	
Sat	
Sun	

Weekly *Review*

WEEK OF ....

CELEBRATE: Write down your wins of the past week (big or small)

1 ....

2 ....

3 ....

REFLECT: What could have gone better?

1 ....

2 ....

3 ....

LEARN: What has this taught you?

1 ....

2 ....

3 ....

WEEKLY REVIEW: How many stars do you give yourself?	**RECOMMIT:** Remind yourself of your big goal. Why are you doing this?
☆ ☆ ☆ ☆ ☆	....

Weekly *Calendar*

MONTH .... YEAR ....

DATE	FINANCIAL MILESTONES, ACTIONS, AND DEADLINES
Mon	
Tue	
Wed	
Thu	
Fri	
Sat	
Sun	

Weekly *Review*

WEEK OF ....

CELEBRATE: Write down your wins of the past week (big or small)

1 ....

2 ....

3 ....

REFLECT: What could have gone better?

1 ....

2 ....

3 ....

LEARN: What has this taught you?

1 ....

2 ....

3 ....

WEEKLY REVIEW: How many stars do you give yourself?

☆ ☆ ☆
☆ ☆

RECOMMIT: Remind yourself of your big goal. Why are you doing this?

....

....

....

Weekly *Calendar*

MONTH .... YEAR ....

DATE	FINANCIAL MILESTONES, ACTIONS, AND DEADLINES
Mon	....
Tue	....
Wed	....
Thu	....
Fri	....
Sat	....
Sun	....

Weekly *Review*

WEEK OF ....

CELEBRATE: Write down your wins of the past week (big or small)

1 ....

2 ....

3 ....

REFLECT: What could have gone better?

1 ....

2 ....

3 ....

LEARN: What has this taught you?

1 ....

2 ....

3 ....

WEEKLY REVIEW: How many stars do you give yourself?

☆ ☆ ☆
☆ ☆

RECOMMIT: Remind yourself of your big goal. Why are you doing this?

....

....

....

Weekly *Calendar*

MONTH .... YEAR ....

DATE	FINANCIAL MILESTONES, ACTIONS, AND DEADLINES
Mon	....
Tue	....
Wed	....
Thu	....
Fri	....
Sat	....
Sun	....

Weekly *Review*

WEEK OF ....

CELEBRATE: Write down your wins of the past week (big or small)

1 ....

2 ....

3 ....

REFLECT: What could have gone better?

1 ....

2 ....

3 ....

LEARN: What has this taught you?

1 ....

2 ....

3 ....

WEEKLY REVIEW: How many stars do you give yourself?

☆ ☆ ☆
☆ ☆

RECOMMIT: Remind yourself of your big goal. Why are you doing this?

....

....

....

Monthly *Review*

MONTH OF ....

Money Mood

☐ upset   ☐ neutral   ☐ excited

WHAT WENT WELL THIS MONTH?

....

....

....

....

THINGS TO DO

STOP DOING ....

....

START DOING ....

....

KEEP DOING ....

....

MY BIGGEST WINS

MY BIGGEST CHALLENGES

MONTHLY SUBGOAL TRACKER

0%   100%

1

2

3

4

5

OTHER REFLECTIONS

Monthly *Net Worth Tracker*

DATE OF REVIEW ....

LAST MONTH'S NET WORTH ....

What you own (assets)
First, gather everything you have:

DESCRIPTION	BALANCE
CASH *(This is your wallet, bank accounts, and any cash you have hidden away)*	
INVESTMENTS *(Things like stocks and retirement accounts)*	
PROPERTY *(Your home or any land you own)*	
BUSINESSES *(If you own a business, even a small one, it counts)*	
OTHER ASSETS *(Anything else that you could sell if you needed to, like a car)*	
TOTAL ASSETS	

What you owe (liabilities)
Now, let's look at what you owe:

DESCRIPTION	BALANCE
HOUSE DEBT *(If you borrowed money to buy your home, e.g., a mortgage)*	
LOANS *(Money you owe for college, a car, or anything else)*	
CREDIT CARD DEBT *(Any expenses you're paying off over time)*	
OTHER DEBTS *(Anything else you might owe)*	
TOTAL LIABILITIES	

MY NET WORTH:
What you own – What you owe

= $ ....

LAST MONTH VS. THIS MONTH

CHANGES IN $	THIS MONTH - LAST MONTH = $ ....
CHANGE IN PERCENTAGE (%)	CHANGE IN $ / LAST MONTH'S NET WORTH = ... %

Monthly *Planning*

MONTH OF ....

SALARY

FIXED INCOME ....

VARIABLE INCOME ....
(BONUS, DIVIDENDS, SIDE HUSTLE, ETC.)

TOTAL INCOME ....

EXPENSES: NECESSITIES (Aim for 50% of your income)

Fill out the budget category at the beginning of the month with what you expect to spend, then fill out the actual category at the end of the month with what you ended up spending.

ITEM	BUDGET	ACTUAL
....	....	....
....	....	....
....	....	....
....	....	....
....	....	....
....	....	....

EXPENSES: FUN (Aim for 30% of your income)

Fill out the budget category at the beginning of the month with what you expect to spend, then fill out the actual category at the end of the month with what you ended up spending.

ITEM	BUDGET	ACTUAL
....	....	....
....	....	....
....	....	....
....	....	....
....	....	....
....	....	....

EXPENSES: FUTURE YOU (Aim for 20% of your income)

Fill out the budget category at the beginning of the month with what you expect to spend, then fill out the actual category at the end of the month with what you ended up spending.

ITEM	BUDGET	ACTUAL
....	....	....
....	....	....
....	....	....
....	....	....

Monthly *Habit Tracker*

MONTH .... **YEAR** ....

LIST YOUR NEW HABITS HERE:

1 ....

2 ....

3 ....

4 ....

5 ....

Mon	*Tue*	*Wed*	*Thu*	*Fri*	*Sat*	*Sun*

Weekly *Calendar*

MONTH .... YEAR ....

DATE	FINANCIAL MILESTONES, ACTIONS, AND DEADLINES
Mon	....
Tue	....
Wed	....
Thu	....
Fri	....
Sat	....
Sun	....

Weekly *Review*

WEEK OF ....

CELEBRATE: Write down your wins of the past week (big or small)

1 ....

2 ....

3 ....

REFLECT: What could have gone better?

1 ....

2 ....

3 ....

LEARN: What has this taught you?

1 ....

2 ....

3 ....

WEEKLY REVIEW: How many stars do you give yourself?

☆ ☆ ☆
☆ ☆

RECOMMIT: Remind yourself of your big goal. Why are you doing this?

....

....

....

Weekly *Calendar*

MONTH .... YEAR ....

DATE	FINANCIAL MILESTONES, ACTIONS, AND DEADLINES
Mon	....
Tue	....
Wed	....
Thu	....
Fri	....
Sat	....
Sun	....

Weekly *Review*

WEEK OF ....

CELEBRATE: Write down your wins of the past week (big or small)

1 ....

2 ....

3 ....

REFLECT: What could have gone better?

1 ....

2 ....

3 ....

LEARN: What has this taught you?

1 ....

2 ....

3 ....

WEEKLY REVIEW: How many stars do you give yourself?

☆ ☆ ☆
☆ ☆

RECOMMIT: Remind yourself of your big goal. Why are you doing this?

....

....

....

Weekly *Calendar*

MONTH .... YEAR ....

DATE	FINANCIAL MILESTONES, ACTIONS, AND DEADLINES
Mon	....
Tue	....
Wed	....
Thu	....
Fri	....
Sat	....
Sun	....

Weekly *Review*

WEEK OF ....

CELEBRATE: Write down your wins of the past week (big or small)

1 ....

2 ....

3 ....

REFLECT: What could have gone better?

1 ....

2 ....

3 ....

LEARN: What has this taught you?

1 ....

2 ....

3 ....

WEEKLY REVIEW: How many stars do you give yourself?

☆ ☆ ☆
☆ ☆

RECOMMIT: Remind yourself of your big goal. Why are you doing this?

....

....

....

Weekly *Calendar*

MONTH .... YEAR ....

DATE	FINANCIAL MILESTONES, ACTIONS, AND DEADLINES
Mon	
Tue	
Wed	
Thu	
Fri	
Sat	
Sun	

Weekly *Review*

WEEK OF ....

CELEBRATE: Write down your wins of the past week (big or small)

1 ....

2 ....

3 ....

REFLECT: What could have gone better?

1 ....

2 ....

3 ....

LEARN: What has this taught you?

1 ....

2 ....

3 ....

WEEKLY REVIEW: How many stars do you give yourself?

☆ ☆ ☆
☆ ☆

RECOMMIT: Remind yourself of your big goal. Why are you doing this?

....

....

....

Monthly *Review*

MONTH OF ....

Money Mood

☐ upset   ☐ neutral   ☐ excited

WHAT WENT WELL THIS MONTH?

THINGS TO DO

STOP DOING ....

START DOING ....

KEEP DOING ....

MY BIGGEST WINS

MY BIGGEST CHALLENGES

MONTHLY SUBGOAL TRACKER

0%   100%

1

2

3

4

5

OTHER REFLECTIONS

Monthly *Net Worth Tracker*

DATE OF REVIEW .... **LAST MONTH'S NET WORTH** ....

What you own (assets)

First, gather everything you have:

DESCRIPTION	BALANCE
CASH *(This is your wallet, bank accounts, and any cash you have hidden away)*	
INVESTMENTS *(Things like stocks and retirement accounts)*	
PROPERTY *(Your home or any land you own)*	
BUSINESSES *(If you own a business, even a small one, it counts)*	
OTHER ASSETS *(Anything else that you could sell if you needed to, like a car)*	
TOTAL ASSETS	

What you owe (liabilities)

Now, let's look at what you owe:

DESCRIPTION	BALANCE
HOUSE DEBT *(If you borrowed money to buy your home, e.g., a mortgage)*	
LOANS *(Money you owe for college, a car, or anything else)*	
CREDIT CARD DEBT *(Any expenses you're paying off over time)*	
OTHER DEBTS *(Anything else you might owe)*	
TOTAL LIABILITIES	

MY NET WORTH:

What you own – What you owe

= $..

LAST MONTH VS. THIS MONTH

CHANGES IN $	THIS MONTH – LAST MONTH = $ ....
CHANGE IN PERCENTAGE (%)	CHANGE IN $ / LAST MONTH'S NET WORTH = ... %

Monthly *Planning*

MONTH OF ....

SALARY

FIXED INCOME ....

VARIABLE INCOME
(BONUS, DIVIDENDS, SIDE HUSTLE, ETC.) ....

TOTAL INCOME ....

EXPENSES: NECESSITIES (Aim for 50% of your income)

Fill out the budget category at the beginning of the month with what you expect to spend, then fill out the actual category at the end of the month with what you ended up spending.

ITEM	BUDGET	ACTUAL
....	....	....
....	....	....
....	....	....
....	....	....
....	....	....
....	....	....

EXPENSES: FUN (Aim for 30% of your income)

Fill out the budget category at the beginning of the month with what you expect to spend, then fill out the actual category at the end of the month with what you ended up spending.

ITEM	BUDGET	ACTUAL

EXPENSES: FUTURE YOU (Aim for 20% of your income)

Fill out the budget category at the beginning of the month with what you expect to spend, then fill out the actual category at the end of the month with what you ended up spending.

ITEM	BUDGET	ACTUAL

Monthly *Habit Tracker*

MONTH .... YEAR ....

LIST YOUR NEW HABITS HERE:

1 ....

2 ....

3 ....

4 ....

5 ....

Mon	*Tue*	*Wed*	*Thu*	*Fri*	*Sat*	*Sun*

Weekly *Calendar*

MONTH .... YEAR ....

DATE	FINANCIAL MILESTONES, ACTIONS, AND DEADLINES
Mon	
Tue	
Wed	
Thu	
Fri	
Sat	
Sun	

Weekly *Review*

WEEK OF ....

CELEBRATE: Write down your wins of the past week (big or small)

1 ....

2 ....

3 ....

REFLECT: What could have gone better?

1 ....

2 ....

3 ....

LEARN: What has this taught you?

1 ....

2 ....

3 ....

WEEKLY REVIEW: How many stars do you give yourself?

☆ ☆ ☆
☆ ☆

RECOMMIT: Remind yourself of your big goal. Why are you doing this?

....

....

....

Weekly *Calendar*

MONTH .... YEAR ....

DATE	FINANCIAL MILESTONES, ACTIONS, AND DEADLINES
Mon	
Tue	
Wed	
Thu	
Fri	
Sat	
Sun	

Weekly *Review*

WEEK OF ....

CELEBRATE: Write down your wins of the past week (big or small)

1 ....

2 ....

3 ....

REFLECT: What could have gone better?

1 ....

2 ....

3 ....

LEARN: What has this taught you?

1 ....

2 ....

3 ....

WEEKLY REVIEW: How many stars do you give yourself?	**RECOMMIT:** Remind yourself of your big goal. Why are you doing this?

☆ ☆ ☆
☆ ☆

....

....

....

Weekly *Calendar*

MONTH .... YEAR ....

DATE	FINANCIAL MILESTONES, ACTIONS, AND DEADLINES
Mon	
Tue	
Wed	
Thu	
Fri	
Sat	
Sun	

Weekly *Review*

WEEK OF ....

CELEBRATE: Write down your wins of the past week (big or small)

1 ....

2 ....

3 ....

REFLECT: What could have gone better?

1 ....

2 ....

3 ....

LEARN: What has this taught you?

1 ....

2 ....

3 ....

WEEKLY REVIEW: How many stars do you give yourself?

☆ ☆ ☆
☆ ☆

RECOMMIT: Remind yourself of your big goal. Why are you doing this?

....

....

....

Weekly *Calendar*

MONTH .... YEAR ....

DATE	FINANCIAL MILESTONES, ACTIONS, AND DEADLINES
Mon	
Tue	
Wed	
Thu	
Fri	
Sat	
Sun	

Weekly *Review*

WEEK OF ....

CELEBRATE: Write down your wins of the past week (big or small)

1 ....

2 ....

3 ....

REFLECT: What could have gone better?

1 ....

2 ....

3 ....

LEARN: What has this taught you?

1 ....

2 ....

3 ....

WEEKLY REVIEW: How many stars do you give yourself?

☆ ☆ ☆
☆ ☆

RECOMMIT: Remind yourself of your big goal. Why are you doing this?

....

....

....

Monthly *Review*

MONTH OF ....

Money Mood

☐ upset   ☐ neutral   ☐ excited

WHAT WENT WELL THIS MONTH?

....

....

....

....

THINGS TO DO

STOP DOING ....

....

START DOING ....

....

KEEP DOING ....

....

MY BIGGEST WINS

MY BIGGEST CHALLENGES

MONTHLY SUBGOAL TRACKER

0%   100%

1

2

3

4

5

OTHER REFLECTIONS

Monthly *Net Worth Tracker*

DATE OF REVIEW .... **LAST MONTH'S NET WORTH** ....

What you own (assets)
First, gather everything you have:

DESCRIPTION	BALANCE
CASH *(This is your wallet, bank accounts, and any cash you have hidden away)*	
INVESTMENTS *(Things like stocks and retirement accounts)*	
PROPERTY *(Your home or any land you own)*	
BUSINESSES *(If you own a business, even a small one, it counts)*	
OTHER ASSETS *(Anything else that you could sell if you needed to, like a car)*	
TOTAL ASSETS	

What you owe (liabilities)
Now, let's look at what you owe:

DESCRIPTION	BALANCE
HOUSE DEBT *(If you borrowed money to buy your home, e.g., a mortgage)*	
LOANS *(Money you owe for college, a car, or anything else)*	
CREDIT CARD DEBT *(Any expenses you're paying off over time)*	
OTHER DEBTS *(Anything else you might owe)*	
TOTAL LIABILITIES	

MY NET WORTH:
What you own – What you owe

= $ ....

LAST MONTH VS. THIS MONTH

CHANGES IN $	THIS MONTH – LAST MONTH = $ ....
CHANGE IN PERCENTAGE (%)	CHANGE IN $ / LAST MONTH'S NET WORTH = ... %

Monthly *Planning*

MONTH OF ....

SALARY

FIXED INCOME ....

VARIABLE INCOME
(BONUS, DIVIDENDS, SIDE HUSTLE, ETC.) ....

TOTAL INCOME ....

EXPENSES: NECESSITIES (Aim for 50% of your income)

Fill out the budget category at the beginning of the month with what you expect to spend, then fill out the actual category at the end of the month with what you ended up spending.

ITEM	BUDGET	ACTUAL
....	....	....
....	....	....
....	....	....
....	....	....
....	....	....
....	....	....

EXPENSES: FUN (Aim for 30% of your income)

Fill out the budget category at the beginning of the month with what you expect to spend, then fill out the actual category at the end of the month with what you ended up spending.

ITEM	BUDGET	ACTUAL

EXPENSES: FUTURE YOU (Aim for 20% of your income)

Fill out the budget category at the beginning of the month with what you expect to spend, then fill out the actual category at the end of the month with what you ended up spending.

ITEM	BUDGET	ACTUAL

Monthly *Habit Tracker*

MONTH .... YEAR ....

LIST YOUR NEW HABITS HERE:

1 ....

2 ....

3 ....

4 ....

5 ....

Mon	*Tue*	*Wed*	*Thu*	*Fri*	*Sat*	*Sun*

Weekly *Calendar*

MONTH .... YEAR ....

DATE	FINANCIAL MILESTONES, ACTIONS, AND DEADLINES
Mon	
Tue	
Wed	
Thu	
Fri	
Sat	
Sun	

Weekly *Review*

WEEK OF ....

CELEBRATE: Write down your wins of the past week (big or small)

1 ....

2 ....

3 ....

REFLECT: What could have gone better?

1 ....

2 ....

3 ....

LEARN: What has this taught you?

1 ....

2 ....

3 ....

WEEKLY REVIEW: How many stars do you give yourself?

☆ ☆ ☆
☆ ☆

RECOMMIT: Remind yourself of your big goal. Why are you doing this?

....

....

....

Weekly *Calendar*

MONTH .... YEAR ....

DATE	FINANCIAL MILESTONES, ACTIONS, AND DEADLINES
Mon	
Tue	
Wed	
Thu	
Fri	
Sat	
Sun	

Weekly *Review*

WEEK OF ....

CELEBRATE: Write down your wins of the past week (big or small)

1 ....

2 ....

3 ....

REFLECT: What could have gone better?

1 ....

2 ....

3 ....

LEARN: What has this taught you?

1 ....

2 ....

3 ....

WEEKLY REVIEW: How many stars do you give yourself?

☆ ☆ ☆
☆ ☆

RECOMMIT: Remind yourself of your big goal. Why are you doing this?

....

....

....

Weekly *Calendar*

MONTH .... YEAR ....

DATE	FINANCIAL MILESTONES, ACTIONS, AND DEADLINES
Mon	
Tue	
Wed	
Thu	
Fri	
Sat	
Sun	

Weekly *Review*

WEEK OF ....

CELEBRATE: Write down your wins of the past week (big or small)

1 ....

2 ....

3 ....

REFLECT: What could have gone better?

1 ....

2 ....

3 ....

LEARN: What has this taught you?

1 ....

2 ....

3 ....

WEEKLY REVIEW: How many stars do you give yourself?

☆ ☆ ☆
☆ ☆

RECOMMIT: Remind yourself of your big goal. Why are you doing this?

....

....

....

Weekly *Calendar*

MONTH .... YEAR ....

DATE	FINANCIAL MILESTONES, ACTIONS, AND DEADLINES
Mon	
Tue	
Wed	
Thu	
Fri	
Sat	
Sun	

Weekly *Review*

WEEK OF ....

CELEBRATE: Write down your wins of the past week (big or small)

1 ....

2 ....

3 ....

REFLECT: What could have gone better?

1 ....

2 ....

3 ....

LEARN: What has this taught you?

1 ....

2 ....

3 ....

WEEKLY REVIEW: How many stars do you give yourself?

☆ ☆ ☆
☆ ☆

RECOMMIT: Remind yourself of your big goal. Why are you doing this?

....

....

....

Monthly *Review*

MONTH OF ....

Money Mood

☐ upset   ☐ neutral   ☐ excited

WHAT WENT WELL THIS MONTH?

....

....

....

....

THINGS TO DO

STOP DOING ....

....

START DOING ....

....

KEEP DOING ....

....

MY BIGGEST WINS

MY BIGGEST CHALLENGES

MONTHLY SUBGOAL TRACKER

0%   100%

1

2

3

4

5

OTHER REFLECTIONS

Year end *reflection*

Congrats! You made it through the past 12 months of reviewing and planning your finances. Good job! Now take a moment to reflect on your success.

1   Did you achieve your financial goals?

YEAR END GOAL	YEAR END PROGRESS

1 ....
....
      0%   100%

2 ....
....
      0%   100%

3 ....
....
      0%   100%

4 ....
....
      0%   100%

5 ....
....
      0%   100%

2 Calculate the change in your net worth:

LAST YEAR VS. THIS YEAR	
CHANGES IN $	***END OF YEAR − **START OF YEAR = $** ....
CHANGE IN %	**CHANGE IN $ /START OF YEAR =** .... **%**

*Use your net worth calculation from page 196   ** Use your net worth calculation from page 15

3 Reflect on the progress you have made over the past 12 months. Did you stay within your means? Did you achieve your goals? Why or why not?

....

....

....

....

....

4 What can you do better next year? Write your motivation.

....

....

....

....

....

Part 3

Bonus: *Enhance your finances*

If you're in a relationship or you just want to kick-start your personal savings, this part is here to help you further improve your financial health to achieve even greater success.

Talk money with *your partner*

Before buying a house, walking down the aisle, or creating a family, it's important to talk about money with your partner. Complete the following financial checklist.

Write down your thoughts separately and share them afterward. Were you aligned, or did anything surprising come up?

---

1 **TALK ABOUT MONEY HONESTLY:** Write down your personal story and beliefs about money or use your answers from the exercise in part 1.

---

2 **SHARE FINANCIAL STRENGTHS, WEAKNESSES, FEARS, AND DREAMS**

Strengths:

Weaknesses: ....

....

....

Fears: ....

....

....

Dreams: ....

....

....

---

3 LAY OUT ALL FINANCIAL INFORMATION: Include income, assets, and debts

TOTAL VALUE OF SALARY ....

TOTAL VALUE OF SAVINGS ....

TOTAL VALUE OF PENSION ....

TOTAL VALUE OF INVESTMENTS ....

TOTAL VALUE OF DEBTS ....

TOTAL VALUE OF OTHER ASSETS ....

4 UNDERSTAND EACH OTHER'S IDEAS ABOUT MONEY: Write down your
financial habits: saving, spending, investing, and giving. Address debt and
your attitude toward it.

....

....

....

....

....

....

....

5 PLAN FOR INCOME DISPARITIES: Consider the following questions before
you combine your finances and assets:

Q: Is all mine, all yours?   **YES**   **NO**

Thoughts: ....

....

Q: Do we need a prenup?   **YES**   **NO**

Thoughts: ....

....

6 SET SHARED GOALS: Write down your future dreams for you and your partner. Differentiate between short-term and long-term financial goals.

7 CREATE A BUDGET AND ASSIGN ROLES: Write down your thoughts on how to split expenses, savings, and spending.

NAME THE MINISTER OF DAY-TO-DAY FINANCES:

NAME THE MINISTER OF LONG-TERM SAVINGS AND/OR INVESTMENTS:

8 TALK ABOUT YOUR FAMILY AND CAREERS: Write down your thoughts about and expectations of family planning, maternity/parental leave, your future career, etc.

Family: ....

....

....

....

Career: ....

....

....

....

Notes: ....

....

....

....

....

....

31-Day Purchasing Freeze

Become more mindful of your spending habits! Avoid making any unnecessary purchases for a whole 31 days.

MONTH .... YEAR ....

TIPS TO STAY ON TRACK

1. **PLAN AHEAD**
   Prepare mentally to resist temptation or avoid it altogether.

2. **AVOID TEMPTATIONS**
   Unsubscribe from marketing emails, and avoid online shopping.

3. **STAY ACTIVE**
   Engage in physical activity to distract yourself.

4. **SEEK SUPPORT**
   Talk to friends or family about your goals and ask them to help you to stay on track.

MY PURCHASING FREEZE MOTIVATION

....

....

....

....

CROSS OUT DAYS WHEN YOU SUCCEED WITH YOUR FREEZE

1	*2*	*3*	*4*	*5*	*6*	*7*	*8*
9	*10*	*11*	*12*	*13*	*14*	*15*	*16*
17	*18*	*19*	*20*	*21*	*22*	*23*	*24*
25	*26*	*27*	*28*	*29*	*30*	*31*	

Save $496 in 31 days

Want to boost your savings? A great way to do it is by saving $496 in just one month. Give it a try and see how much you can achieve. Good luck!

My action steps:

- ☐ ....
- ☐ ....
- ☐ ....
- ☐ ....
- ☐ ....
- ☐ ....
- ☐ ....
- ☐ ....
- ☐ ....
- ☐ ....
- ☐ ....
- ☐ ....
- ☐ ....
- ☐ ....
- ☐ ....

DAY	DEPOSIT	BALANCE	DONE
1	$1	$1	☐
2	$2	$3	☐
3	$3	$6	☐
4	$4	$10	☐
5	$5	$15	☐
6	$6	$21	☐
7	$7	$28	☐
8	$8	$36	☐
9	$9	$45	☐
10	$10	$55	☐
11	$11	$66	☐
12	$12	$78	☐
13	$13	$91	☐
14	$14	$105	☐
15	$15	$120	☐
16	$16	$136	☐
17	$17	$153	☐
18	$18	$171	☐
19	$19	$190	☐
20	$20	$210	☐
21	$21	$231	☐
22	$22	$253	☐
23	$23	$276	☐
24	$24	$300	☐
25	$25	$325	☐
26	$26	$351	☐
27	$27	$378	☐
28	$28	$406	☐
29	$29	$435	☐
30	$30	$465	☐
31	$31	$496	☐

Saving for ....

Do you have a specific savings goal in mind?
Regardless of what it may be, decide on an end date and
make a commitment to set aside one-twelfth of the required
amount at regular intervals until you reach your goal.

MY GOAL ....

MY MOTIVATION ....

	DATE	AMOUNT
1	....	....
2	....	....
3	....	....
4	....	....
5	....	....
6	....	....
7	....	....
8	....	....
9	....	....
10	....	....
11	....	....
12	....	....

END DATE ....   **TOTAL** ....

Congratulations. *You did it!*

As you close this chapter of your financial journey, remember that every number, goal, and decision made in the past 12 months tells a story of hard work, dedication, and consistency. Money is more than just cash in the bank; it reflects your choices, values, and dreams.

The small steps, daily choices, and commitment to your goals are what truly make a difference.

So congratulate yourself on achieving your goals! This is a major accomplishment that deserves to be celebrated. Take some time to reflect on all the hard work and dedication that went into making this happen.

Consider the habits that were developed along the way and how they can be maintained in the future to ensure continued success. Don't rest on your laurels; the coming year presents new opportunities to challenge yourself and set even higher goals. So reflect on the lessons learned from this achievement and apply them to your upcoming financial goals.

Remember, success is a journey, not a destination.

Feeling like you've fallen short of some goals can be discouraging, but take heart! Setting high standards shows your ambition and drive to succeed, which is something to be proud of. Instead of being too critical of yourself, try channeling that energy into moving forward.

You can also use this opportunity positively to assess what worked and what didn't, and to make adjustments accordingly. Remember, each new day brings with it a chance to make better choices and learn from yesterday's mistakes.

It's important to keep in mind that the journey to achieving your dreams may be tough, but with determination, perseverance, and a positive attitude, you can overcome any obstacle in your way.

So keep pushing forward, and never give up on your aspirations!

We are rooting for you every step of the way.

Camilla, Anna & Emma

Sources
4 Katie Donegan, Interview with Female Invest, "I Retired at 35—Here's How I Used the FIRE Method to Do It," March 3, 2023, **18** Anne Sweeney, event at Stanford University, November 4, 2013, **29** Adapted from *Atomic Habits* by James Clear (p.50). Published by Avery, 2018, Penguin Random House, **40** Sheryl Sandberg, *Lean In: Women, Work, and the Will to Lead*, Knopf (2013)

Publisher's acknowledgments
DK would like to thank Monika Memytė and Julie Otzen for design development work.

DK UK

Editorial Director Cara Armstrong
Project Editor Izzy Holton
Senior Designer Tania Gomes
Managing Editor Ruth O'Rourke
Senior Production Editor Tony Phipps
US Senior Editor Jennette ElNaggar
Senior Production Controller Luca Bazzoli
Jacket and Sales Material Coordinator Emily Cannings
Art Director Max Pedliham
Publishing Director Katie Cowan

Editorial Helena Caldon
Design Bess Daly

First American Edition, 2024
Published in the United States by DK Publishing
1745 Broadway, 20th Floor, New York, NY 10019

Copyright © 2024 Dorling Kindersley Limited
DK, a Division of Penguin Random House LLC
24 25 26 27 28 10 9 8 7 6 5 4 3 2 1
001–342373–May/2024

Text copyright © Camilla Falkenberg, Emma Due Bitz, and Anna-Sophie Hartvigsen 2024

Camilla Falkenberg, Emma Due Bitz, and Anna-Sophie Hartvigsen have asserted their rights to be identified as the authors of this work.

A catalog record for this book is available from the Library of Congress.
ISBN 978-0-5938-4615-5

Printed and bound in China

www.dk.com

This book was made with Forest Stewardship Council™ certified paper—one small step in DK's commitment to a sustainable future.
For more information go to www.dk.com/our-green-pledge